Late Nights On Venus

AF624549

Kewayne Wadley

BookLeaf Publishing

Presentation by *BookLeaf Publishing*

Web: www.bookleafpub.com

E-mail: info@bookleafpub.com

ISBN: 9789357440516

First edition 2023

DEDICATION

For lovers & dreamers everywhere;

Your rocket ship awaits

ACKNOWLEDGEMENT

To everyone at BookLeaf Publishing I am honored to be a part of this amazing project.

To my family: My Grandmother & Grandfather, Linda Clark and Johnnie Clark Jr for always encouraging me to keep going and not being afraid to start what ever it is that my heart desires.
I love you both dearly!
My Mother and Father, Wayne and Keneethia Wadley for all the extra love and providing me with the gift of life. I love you dearly!
My Baby Brother, Tevin Wadley. You're still the baby! But I love your outlook on life. You may be taller but I still have the looks. Love you bro!
My eldest brother, Erik Mann. I love you and appreciate you for our long talks on how to improve not just self but the environment that we surround ourselves with. Love you!
My brother, Joshua Bivens. Thanks bro for giving a different perspective. We may have all inherited different gifts. By far I wish I had your determination. Love you!

To my friends: Cammry Lapka, thank you for always being yourself. It may have only been a couple of years but I consider it a treasure to have met you, there are still plenty of memories to make.
To Derek Perry, Thank you bro for always being there. You may not have known it, but even on my

brightest day you kept me motivated to keep going. You still do.

To Jeremy Allen, you my friend are something else. Ok no jokes, had to get it out of my system. I appreciate you amigo for always being able to separate self from what ever situation that was going on around you. When I think of you. One word comes to mind. Righteous. Keep doing what you're doing hermano.

To Alice Branch, sometimes life happens & when it does there is a bright light that comes out of nowhere. That is where you enter stage right and steal the show. Thank you so much.

To Donna Ballard Carter, I remember when we first met. I was 22. You helped me to see the bigger picture and pushed me to if nothing else, at least try just as everyone has. You're an amazing friend and I appreciate you for always being there. Even though you sometimes have the habit of disappearing. Kidding.

To my work family: Justin Brody, Lee Esther, Mary Morrow, Brian Travers, Bridget Monroe, Shelia Johnson, Victor Temple, Stanley Neville, Paula Monroe, Christopher Key, Robert Lee, Linda Fields, LaVita Lewis, Christy Mays, Cordney Brown, David Gerald Kelly, Justin Chism, Jerry Duckett, Dylan Cheeks, Margaret Harris, John Powell, Mark Singleton, Cornelius Jackson, Willie White, Frank Orsby, Timothy Newell, Patrick Sager, Ronnie Thomas, Marco Crum, Paul Strong, Jeffrey Ricketts, Kim Harris, Janet Meriwether Price, Joan Brown

You all are my brothers and sisters. I really appreciate the way that you all have come into my life. For all of the memories & lessons that you've taught me & continue to teach. I will forever be grateful and it's a pleasure to be able to call you all my extended family. Thank you for always being there

Tell Me

Tell me about your day
While we sit on the couch &
I lay my head on your lap.
Moment after moment.
Seeing you smile makes my day
That much brighter.
A language that I've grown
Accustom to learn.
The way you vocalize &
Wrap your words not just my ears
But my soul.
How honest & sincere they are.
I stand on the balcony of your lap
& stare into the sun of your eyes

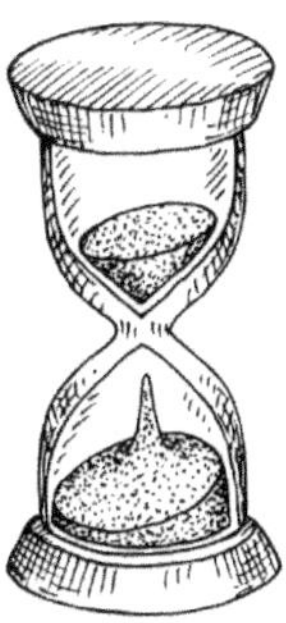

Notifications

The only notification I want to see
Flash across my screen has your name
Highlighted with a heart.
I know that there are more important
Things to be considered in respect to life,
But when it comes to you
I hate saying goodbye.
Whether in person or tapping my thumbs
On a tempered screen.
Although technology has made some things
A bit easier,
This hasn't been one of them.
Driving out to the country
Where there isn't a strong enough signal
& surprising you with a notification
That can't be set with a call or text.
Your tongue is the port
that brings me back to life

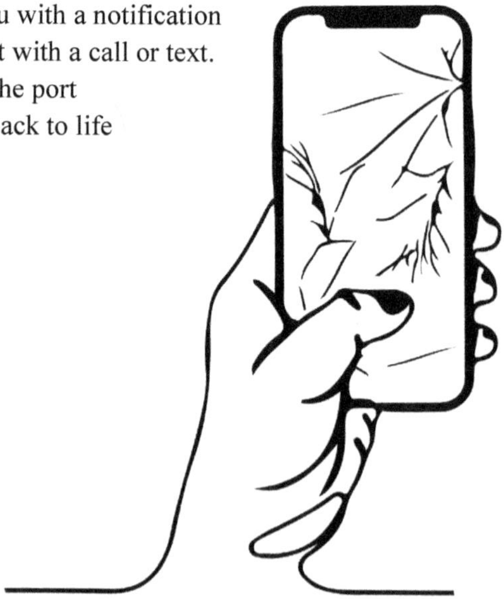

Journaling

I've told a journal how I feel about you,
Out of fear of how you'd react
In the event of telling you.
Through past experiences, the happiest
Times I've had occurred when I kept them
To myself.
I've told this journal everything about you &
We've traveled page after page
In endless vacation.
How we've experienced things we both thought
We'd never experience.
How the food you normally scrunch your nose up at
Turned out to be some of the best things
you ever tasted & how badly I wanted
to be laid out on that plate.
To be the reason you sit back and undo the top
Button on your jeans.
The reason you tell your friends to come visit,
Your return trip back.
I've told a journal how I feel about you,
Out of fear of how you'd react.
Once I tell you, the you that I've come
To know and love will no longer be existent
& all I'll have is another journal entry

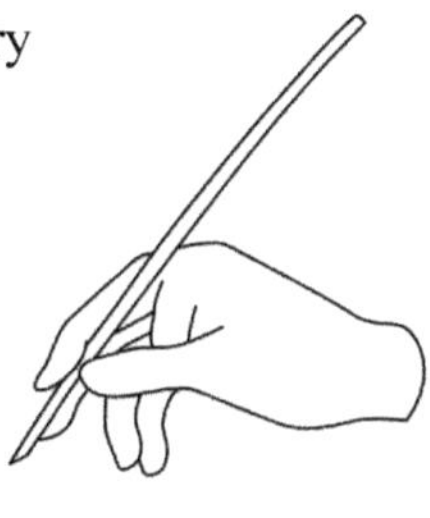

A Poem For Van

The first time I truly saw the stars
In front of me was in the eyes of someone
That truly cared for & about me.

They were so big, I saw my reflection
And everything behind me.
Before that moment they were always
So far away.

Astronomers definitely got it wrong
As far as being anatomically correct.
They were so round & perfect,
At that moment it feels like I could
Have drawn them.

There isn't a street light
Or a city in existence that could compare.
She kissed me & gave me a memory
That I'll always remember.

Compared to her everything else
Seemed small.
Until this day it still does.
I continue to search the sky for her
Again & again

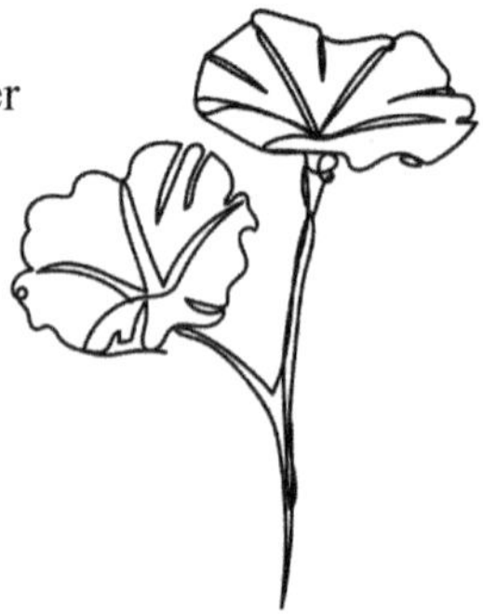

Cigarette Butts

When it comes to you
I cannot help myself or the way
That my teeth love to mark on you.
Just the thought of exploring every inch
Of you.
Flicking my tongue against you.
When love bites, sometimes you bite back.
An invitation sent solely by lips,
Desire being the aggressor between you & I.
Welcoming you & my tongue to become
The best of roommates.
The taste of your body drives me wild.
Cause for bruises that throb for more than normality.
How soft you are between my lips.
How easily you take my mind off of everything.
I am tongue tied at the thought of you

Does Heaven Allow Carry-ons?

She wandered into my heart &
At that moment the blood refused to pump
All of the different offices began to quit.
I felt a terrible pain in my chest
Beginning to cough.
Over time, she's wandered all over my body.
At times she lets me know where she is
By dancing.
My many organs have cried out, stating
That she needs to go.
That, either she leaves or they will all
Protest and quit.
I've attempted to explain to them
that no matter what, change is inevitable.
That no matter what. Something is bound to
Change.
I now wander in eternal ecstasy
Carrying her with me.
Everywhere I go

Look or Sound

We watch and quote our favorite movies
All of the time.
You indulge in all the goofy things
That I believe are funny,
Split right down the middle.
I love laughing with you.
So much that I've lost count of all the
Silly faces we make.
To me it doesn't matter
If the world thinks that I am funny or not.
Deep down I'll always wonder why you laugh
The way that you do & generally mean it.
It's like I am in my own personal heaven
When I am around you.
Admittedly, I never thought about how crazy
Or weird I looked while letting out
an unrestrained laugh.
But if it counts, there is no one else
I'd rather share these laughs with.
No matter how crazy we may look or sound.
It's always you

Faith

I know that there are things that I've done
That you despise me for;
Despicable things. Mainly the way that
I've made you feel the duration of getting
To know you.
While everything will feel like an cop put
& saying sorry is like salt to an open wound.
It's important that you know
Of all things that it was nothing that you've done.
Of all of the times you've questioned yourself
It's important that you know that it was not on you solely.
My attention was always yours.
You are more than capable.
At times it felt that you took my kindness for weakness
On top of all the stress suffered from work.
When it boils down to it.
You made me feel incapable when I indeed made time for you,
You blew me off.
When I attempted to hold on to you,
You made our own needs priority & my voice became
Smaller & smaller,
I couldn't open up and communicate none of this with you.

I wasn't allowed to.
Your sister, your friends.
Your ego took what was thought to be my place,
And when they made you upset I was the first place
You came to, to release that stress.
You never took the time to place yourself in my shoes
And wanted more than any human being could give.
Tipping the scale to its breaking point.
It is through you that I was able to correct myself.
It is through us that I learned faith

Seen Your Face Before

Falling in love with you is like being
Alone on a beautiful island.
You get lost exploring everything
That you possibly can.
The breeze brushing against
Your face.
The first thought being,
I wish I lived somewhere like this.
To experience the tropics
In the summer no matter what time
Of the year.
The sunset reaches down to caress
The ocean, calm in its embrace.
Sand covered feet surrounded
by palm trees.
Falling in love with you is like
Remembering a dream you spoke
To someone you've never seen.
Then having the same dream
The next night growing attached
Not knowing when you're going
To wake up.
To find that it wasn't a dream

Rose Sitting in a Glass of Water

I love how we can just sit & talk
About anything.
Most times when I get quiet
I am thinking about everything
Outside of the moment,
As much freedom as we have
With each other.
How much do we really hide from
Each other? If anything?
When I look at you
I've found the perfect reason to
Smile.
As we both stare up at the sky.
One day we'll both be old
& when we're old how many memories
Of each other will we truly remember?
My hand like a root attached to yours.
Unfortunately time has a selfish
Tendency to weave through
The garden of life
& when that time comes.
I'll look back at these times
And remember you as the rose
That sat on my table in a glass

Of water,
& how much life we've both poured
Into each other

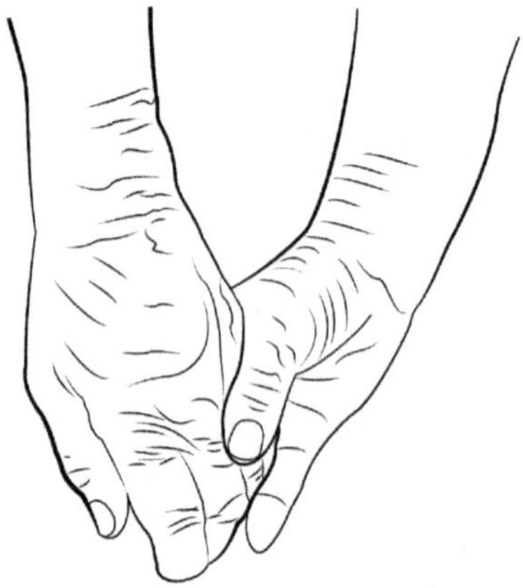

Goodnight

I miss being out late wandering
Around the city streets with you.
Lost in the city lights.
Looking for something to do,
Watching the other cars pass by
Us as we pass by them.
Ignoring all the signs of goodnight
As pretty much everything
Is getting ready to close.
All we were in search of was
For something to do,
Somewhere to go.
My curiosity mingling with yours.
Most nights it felt like a dream
Being able to spend that time
With you.
Most nights it still does.
I can still hear your voice

Something So Small

With the millions and trillions of sparks
that light the sky.
I sat and wished upon
the brightest one that I saw.
Not once did I ever think that it would stop
Not once did I ever think that anything planetary
would listen to something so small,
So meek.
A prayer sincere in meaning.
Two physical beings wanting connect on a
spiritual plane.
The manifestation of deep longing, burning
bright in the sky.
Law of attraction causing mass commotion
amongst the other stars.
A representative of deep stares, the connection
of eyes.
Revealing how big you truly are.
A curious question, would you accept me as I
am?
The slightest touch of hearts orbiting a single
thought that leads to many.
The compilation of stars appearing smaller the
closer you get.
Arms stretching wider welcoming your embrace.

A fragile thing

In all honesty,
I'll drown in you forever if it means I'll never get this close to you again.

Ice Cream Sundae

If you could be anything I'd like you to be an ice
cream sundae.
Layered to perfection.
A picture perfect representation of how I see you.
Extra fudge drenched from each edge of the bowl.
Scandalous, the way you'd lay.
Extra cherries sitting on top of your head.
How devilishly sexy that would be.
Inviting ourselves to be selfish with no end to how
many
spoonfuls we'd take of each other.
Quenching need with melted thirst.
Devoured in everlasting bliss.
The lips that long to taste every inch of you.
Until the bowl is no more

Thelonious Monk

Make me something good to eat
Make me something good to eat.
I don't just want something good
I want something extraordinarily
Good.

I want something that feeds
A hungry soul;
Warm & inviting.
Like coming home to a warm
House on a cold day.
A stranger on the street that does
Something for somebody just
Because.

Burgers, fries, a seafood gumbo,
Fettuccini & shrimp pasta.
I want to feel the orchestra
I'm my stomach come alive
When they begin to play their
Favorite part.
The slide of a trombone that hits
The right note at the precise time.
A tender morsel dressed in it's
Best attempting to keep composure.

That good friend that comes in
Unexpectedly.
Unintentionally unnoticed,
Invited in with open arms in quiet
Suspense.
Finding something you didn't know
You were missing

Wine Tasting

Tonight
I'll have whatever you're having
Let's fill our glasses
With something that we both
Can believe in.
Something that symbolizes
How we feel in each other's arms.
Something like your eyes &
The way that they reflect
Oblivion.
I get lost in them,
Sometimes undress in them.
Salivating in the way that you
Swish around my mouth.
You've filled my glass
With strawberry wine &
Danced around the realm of
What is art & what is nature.
Posing in anyway that you wish
Your body is like fluid in my hands.
Let's fill our glasses
With something we both
Can believe in.
I've never seen your cheeks
Blossom the way that they have

Tonight.
I've grabbed you by the stem &
I've stumbled down the hallway
Of your heart
& Passed right out careful
not to spill a drop

What's for Dinner

I have run from you
One time too many
Finding myself out in the open,
There aren't too many places
To hide.
I've slid between the spaces
Of your fork
& Now you have me pinned.
I have run from you one time too many
I hope that you have mercy on me.
Along the lines of patience
I realize that mercy may be asking too much
But until now I've realized how big your teeth
Really are.
With no place to run & your fork fast-ly
Approaching there is nowhere else on this Plate to
run.
I have run from you one time too many
But after tasting your lips.
I question myself,
Why did I run in the first place

Banana

She was like a banana.
The best part of her was on the inside.
The amount of insulin I'd need trying to devour her whole.
God knows how much I love the thought of that.
The effect she has on me.
Each time I see her I'd unravel her piece by piece until all of her was shown.
The only problem was that I was allergic to bananas.
Although her smell was intoxicating.
One taste and my throat would instantly swell.
Though I wouldn't prefer anything else.
I revealed all of this to her
and she laughed.
She laughed her ass off as a matter of fact.
Rocking back and forth.
Her little brown shoes clicking together.
Her yellow skin now, a bit red.
Her freckles now in full view.
When I asked why she laughed as hard as
She did, she said it's quite alright
Relieving any doubt that I had.
Most people I've met speak so highly of themselves she stated,

But you're the first person I think I'll ever openly admit this to.
You correctly know how to open a banana

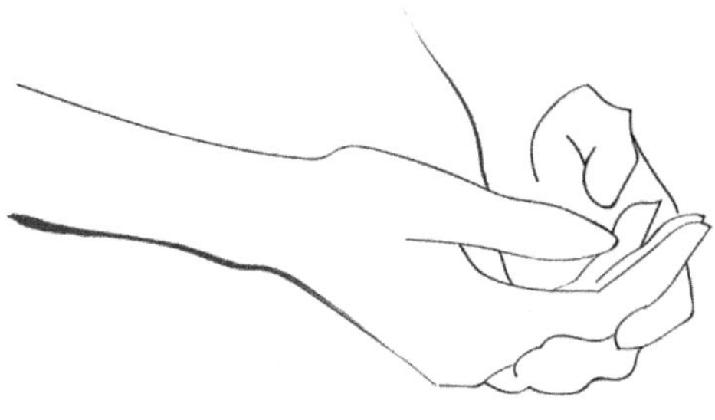

Love of my Life

In today's world it's easy to lose track of time
& otherwise get caught up in what's going on.
So many families split up, so many loved ones
Lose track of who they are. Why they came together.
Divorcing a memory they can never truly run away from.
In today's world it's a blessing to know you. To get facial recognition & assurance with your every smile.
Not every moment can be as perfect as we expect it,
Yet we are appreciative and try not to take the moment
For granted. Just as the saying goes, "Not everyone knows what
They have." It's those refreshing moments that remind us
Of God's praise. Not at all excusing us for the times we become
Absentees when we're needed most, or simply lose track
Of time, there are so many things that factor into who we are,

Our upbringing, things we experience, The
shapeless void
Of a missing father.

While that effect is monumental, we respond
without responding.
Silence sometimes the most powerful form of
toxicity
In response to communication.
In today's world it's not that uncommon, placing
something else
Instead as priority, forgetting the bigger if not
biggest issue.
For better or worse, the most memorable part of
any union.
We take it at face value forgetting that we're all
kids at some point
Or another. It's not impossible to revert back as
we're all human
At the end of the day.
That doesn't at all excuse us for the times we
aren't present,
not just for ourselves. But for our partners, our
friends, our families
the priority of accepting love as a walking and
breathing testimony.
Our hands the door of faith, as we journey to the
alter our lips
Have formed.

In today's world it's a blessing to know you & to get facial recognition
As well as reassurance every time I look at you.
No matter how much we mumble or grumble. I am forever grateful
to have met the love of my life.
Everything I'll ever need no matter how much time passes.
You're all I'll ever need

Strike Twice

If I stay still long enough
It's bound to happen.
It goes by in a blink,
Sometimes hard to catch
But truth is if you believe in it
Than anything is possible.
Sometimes lightening can be vulnerable.
A daffodil dancing in a field of rain.
It goes by in a blink,
If I stay long enough.
Then it's bound to happen.
& as soon as it does I'll twist the top
Back on the jar.
Thought to be the safest place possible.
I wasn't looking for you, but that's
How the best miracles happen
No matter how imperfect, we both are
electrified.
Thought to be the safest place possible.
I put the lid on top of my head
& waited for you to strike the second time
around.
Deliriously absorbed in ecstasy
Edison would be proud

City of Angels

Truth, a five letter word for distinction.
Sometimes I feel I am losing sleep.
Dreaming of a good deed, one day sooner
or later.
Not enough sleep, not enough good places
to go.
I know of one place.
I lost my keys one day last week.
An apartment filled with desire, blinding
lights
& a halo up on a hill.
Further up the road I found my good deed
For little or nothin'
For the first time in a long time I laid & I slept
for hours.
Finding myself beside you,
That one uninvited feeling after a million and
one
Bad invited feelings.
One day baby I am gonna thank you
One day baby you'll see.
I'll feed you from a bowl where everything
Will be alright.
One day, sooner or later.
The latter a beautiful mystique disguised

Under a halo.
One day, sooner or later.
I'll find those keys & escape the boundaries
That live in my mind.
One day soon baby, I'll get on my knees
& accept you as the truth I've known all along

Rocket Love

Sky's the limit as dreams expand.
Tonight let's touch the sky.
Surpassing the clouds that hinder our view.
Hold on to me as the minutes work overtime.
Rushing into the infinity of every touch.
Our sigh stains the orbit of space.
Our arch now, off the ground
Soaring past the stars.
Paradise awaits
As my body fills yours.
A gasp breaks the silence.
I've never seen the moon glow as brightly as it has.
A supernova of bliss implodes.
Casting stones all around us.
Debris of residue subsides.
Uncovering the eclipse of your eyes.
The sweetest nectar fills our lips as our bodies move in unison.
Soaring towards the moon.
Venus aligns perfectly with Mars.
Casting worry into the asteroids, soon to collide.
Just as you and I.
Soon to plant the flag into
the moon's surface

www.ingramcontent.com/pod-product-compliance
Lightning Source LLC
Chambersburg PA
CBHW051748130826
49812CB00033B/1056
9789357440516